ERIC WALTERS

FROM THE HEART OF AFRICA

A BOOK OF WISDOM

tundra

I often say to students, "Raise your hand if you're African." I then tell them that they all should have raised their hands because we're all African. Whether you believe in a religious or scientific explanation, Africa is where we all started our journey on this planet. One people, one race, one place. It's from this home that we began and then fanned out across the world.

This is also where our wisdom began. Our collective knowledge that developed and evolved started with our first ancestors. Without them, there would be no Socrates or Plato, Confucius or Buddha, Einstein or Edison, Gandhi or Mandela, Michelangelo or Da Vinci. To paraphrase Sir Isaac Newton, "We stand on the shoulders of the giants who came before us." Those first giants lived in Africa.

I co-founded and co-run an organization called Creation of Hope (www.creationofhope.com). Our program is focused on the Mbooni District in Kenya, and every year I spend time with the orphans who live in our residence, as well as in the community and in the schools. I consider them and the people who run the program to be family. Presently we have 59 children in the residence; over 75 in high school, college, university or trade school placements; and we support many more orphans and impoverished children who live with extended family members. Our program provides direct support to these children, pays tuition fees, creates water projects, has built a library, operates a school for preschool teachers and provides monthly food, instrumental assistance and supplies to orphans and impoverished children throughout the region. It is important to state that decisions are made on the ground in Kenya by the committee that oversees the program. While both my wife and I have a place on this committee, we constitute two of ten members with the other members being people from the community. This program belongs to the people of Mbooni District and is guided by those trusted community elders. We firmly believe that programs for Kenyans need to be run by Kenyans.

This book is a collection of aphorisms that I've heard from African friends and colleagues over the time I've spent there. I consider these people to be some of the wisest and most intelligent I've ever met, and hearing these aphorisms from them helped me understand their perspectives and their worldviews—and taught me so much! It has been my great privilege and honor to have been taken in by this community and to have been made an elder.

Because aphorisms are an oral tradition, it's hard to pinpoint exactly where they originated. They're also often shared by different cultures in different countries, and like any great wisdom, they've traveled far and wide. But we've done our best to track down where they came from, and we hope that this truly universal wisdom speaks to everyone.

I'm thrilled to say that a portion of my royalties from this book will be donated to the orphans of Creation of Hope to help provide for their education, and Penguin Random House Canada will be matching that donation.

I hope you will both enjoy and learn from these sayings, and remember: we are all African.

With great thanks,
Eric Walters

Foreword

Aphorisms, or proverbs, like the ones in this book, are a kind of portable knowledge about every situation: sayings that give guidance and instruction for life's issues. Aphorisms occur in all human societies, but they are especially common in previously orally based societies like most that are found in Africa.

At the heart of an aphorism is observation. Someone would see a situation and its solution, and then work them into a memorable phrase or mini story. Then the aphorism would be created: written in poetic form or in song, beaten in drums or played with flutes, but mostly just spoken. The person who created the aphorism wasn't credited or mentioned, and a lot of times, the original situation wasn't mentioned either. What was important was the sharing of the helpful information.

Aphorisms are shared as a way to help someone make a decision or find a solution to a problem. They are used as a way to communicate: to make arguments and defend ideas, settle quarrels and find common ground; as a form of entertainment; and as a way to praise a person or community. In the African tradition, the aphorisms in this book are a way to share the collective knowledge of the community through art and story.

African children begin to learn aphorisms from a very young age. Their elders use the aphorisms as a way to help the children understand an issue. And in African societies with rites of passage where customs, songs and other lore are taught, aphorisms are included as a way to share the wisdom of the community with the younger generation.

Aphorisms are a flexible and versatile form of communication, and the knowledge within them is universal. They collect a wealth of historical experience in one simple package that can be used by anyone and in any situation to help chart a way forward. They are a traditional form of communication that continues to be used to this day, and though the knowledge and insight contained in them may have begun in Africa—as the cradle of human beings—they aren't limited to Africa. The same aphorism might be found in Sweden that is found in Kenya—with perhaps a few modifications!

While aphorisms have been compiled in written forms all over the world, as living art forms they generally reside in the African memory, ready to be drawn upon and shared at appropriate moments.

It is commendable that Eric Walters is bringing this short selection of African aphorisms, with their timeless and universal wisdom, to the notice of an increasingly fast-paced world that in some ways is losing its connections with roots and customs. This celebration of art and knowledge is a way to slow down and appreciate this ancient but always relevant art form.

Eric has been involved in human and community development initiatives in East Africa for over a decade. His organization Creation of Hope holds to a philosophy to help people solve their own problems in the most effective, practicable and indigenous way possible. Creation of Hope offers its support but doesn't dictate how things should be done. This is an empowering philosophy. Aphorisms are a way for children to learn not only knowledge, but language, and by publishing this book, Eric and Creation of Hope are helping the children in their orphanage and the community become more literate. Through the aphorisms they can learn wisdom; through the sales of the book their education will be secured.

Dr. Femi Kolapo
Associate Professor of African History
History Department, University of Guelph

When in the middle of a river, do not insult the crocodile.

ORIGIN: BAOULÉ PEOPLE, CÔTE D'IVOIRE

MEANING: Wait until you're on the riverbank and out of harm's way before you make a crocodile angry! You probably don't have to battle crocodiles, but you can apply this to any situation: always think before you act.

Traveling is learning.

ORIGIN: KIKUYU PEOPLE, KENYA

MEANING: There is so much to learn from other people and other cultures! But you don't need to leave home to learn about others—get to know people in your neighborhood who are different from you and you'll see the world from a new perspective. You can learn from their travels!

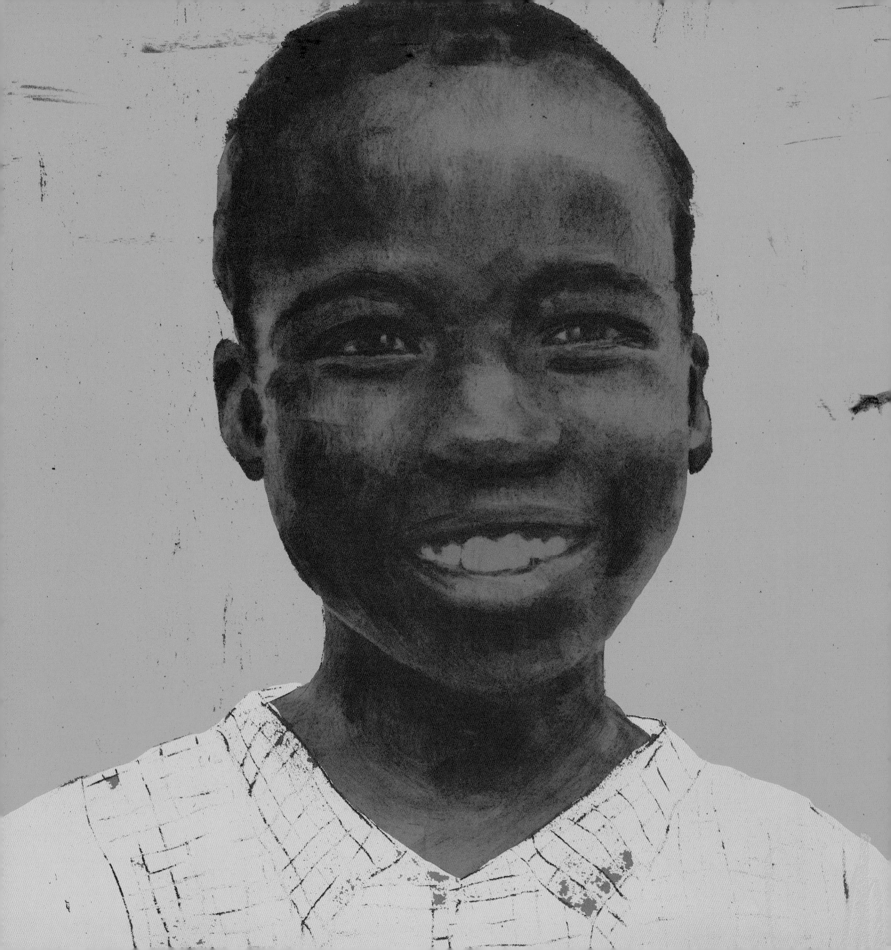

Children are the reward of life.

ORIGIN: BAKONGO PEOPLE, CENTRAL AFRICA

MEANING: Community is very important, and children are a big part of any community. You are pretty special! Everything your parents, your grandparents and everyone else who came before you learned gets passed down, so those ancestors live on through you.

I pointed out to you the stars, but all you saw was the tip of my finger.

ORIGIN: SUKUMA PEOPLE, TANZANIA

MEANING: Don't focus only on the small things or just what's in front of you—look around and see the bigger picture. If you have an open mind, you will see and learn so much more.

It takes a village to raise a child.

ORIGIN: THE IGBO (NIGERIA) AND YORUBA (NIGERIA AND BENIN REPUBLIC), WEST AFRICA

MEANING: Children are not raised just by their parents. Siblings, grandparents, aunts and uncles, friends and the larger community all play a role in educating and caring for a child.

You must judge a man by the work of his hands.

ORIGIN: NORTHERN AFRICA

MEANING: Sometimes we judge people based on how they look, but we should judge people by what they do, instead. Doing good things is more important than appearance.

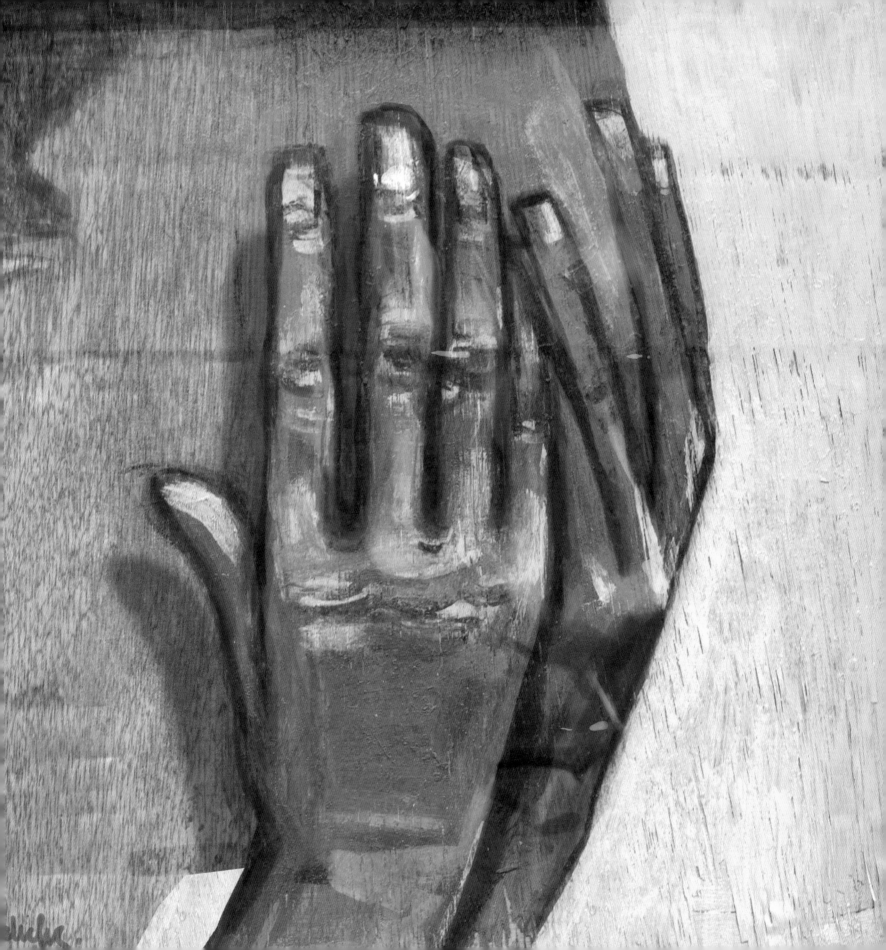

Do not follow the path. Go to where there is no path to begin the trail.

ORIGIN: ASHANTI PEOPLE, GHANA

MEANING: Be brave, be yourself and remember that you don't always have to do what others are doing. Sometimes doing your own thing is the most rewarding.

No one tests the depth of the water with both feet.

ORIGIN: EWE PEOPLE, WEST AFRICA

MEANING: Think about jumping into a river with both feet: you're already in the river before you know how deep it is, and it might be over your head! So carefully judge a situation before you dive headlong into it, and you'll know you're making the right choice.

Many hands make light work.

ORIGIN: HAYA PEOPLE, TANZANIA

MEANING: Imagine trying to lift a very heavy boulder: alone, it would be hard. But with many people, it would be much easier. Cooperation in any aspect of life makes things easier, and more fun!

Rain does not fall on one roof alone.

ORIGIN: CAMEROON

MEANING: There's never just one cloud raining on one person, and you're never really alone. Whatever you're feeling or experiencing, someone else probably has too. Both sorrow and good fortune are often shared by many. By being kind and open to those around you, you'll experience that kindness back, and you might just solve your problems together!

There's always a winner, even in a monkey's beauty contest.

ORIGIN: KENYA

MEANING: Someone always wins, even when the competition isn't important! Don't attach too much value to things just because they've been judged to be the best. Use your own mind to decide what YOU think is best.

The longest journey starts with a single footstep.

ORIGIN: AFRICAN PROVERB

MEANING: Every journey has a beginning and an end, and often the hardest part is at the start. Sometimes tasks seem too big, but by taking just one step, you're one step closer to achieving success.

If you wish to go fast, go alone. If you wish to go far, go together.

ORIGIN: N'GAMBAY PEOPLE, CENTRAL AFRICA

MEANING: If you need to get somewhere fast, going alone means no one will slow you down. But if you're alone, you might be stopped by obstacles that you can't overcome without help.

Wisdom is like the baobab tree: no one person can embrace it.

ORIGIN: EWE PEOPLE, WEST AFRICA

MEANING: No one person can know all there is to know. Our brains are just too small!

There is so much wisdom in the world, we all have to keep small pieces of it—and always share!

Unity is strength.

ORIGIN: GANDA PEOPLE, UGANDA

MEANING: If we all support each other and stick together, we become a team.

And when we rally together as a team, we can do so much more than each of us can alone.

Setor Fiadzigbey is an illustrator and former aircraft trainee engineer from Accra, Ghana. He's been drawing all his life, and he was nominated for the Golden Baobab Prize and the Kuenyehia Prize. ↓

↑ **Rogé** is a French Canadian artist who worked in advertising before turning to illustration, painting and writing. He has twice won the Governor General's Literary Award and numerous others. He lives in Quebec.

Toby Newsome lives and works in Cape Town, South Africa. He designs and illustrates, and he works in mixed media. He plays guitar, but strictly for relaxation purposes! ↓

Xanelé Purén is a South African illustrator and designer and co-founder of See Saw Do, a spatial and interactive design studio. She won the Golden Baobab Prize, and she has a cat named Bob. ↓

← **Tom Gonzalez** was born in Havana, Cuba, and now lives in Duluth, Georgia. He's been an art director, principal designer and creative development manager; he's been an artist his whole life.

← **Maaike Bakker** is an illustrator, exhibition curator, lecturer and fine artist from Pretoria, South Africa. Maaike has been illustrating for ten years and works mainly in Illustrator and Photoshop.

↑ **Joe Morse** is an award-winning illustrator and the Coordinator of the Bachelor of Illustration Program at Sheridan College Oakville, Ontario. He lives in Toronto.

CLPE poetry book award–winner **Iain McIntosh** was born in Motherwell, Scotland, and now lives in Edinburgh. He uses scratchboard, pen on paper and a digital tablet, and he's been illustrating since the 1980s. →

← TD Award winner and Governor General's Award nominee **Melinda Josie** grew up in Muskoka, Ontario. She has been drawing and painting as long as she can remember, and she works mostly in watercolor. She lives in Toronto.

↑ **Elicser Elliott** is a Toronto-based street artist whose famous aerosol murals appear all over the city. He was born in Montreal, Quebec, and grew up in the West Indies (St. Vincent). He's been an artist for 21 years.

← Award-winning artist **Eugenie Fernandes** was born on a big island (Long Island, New York) and now lives on a little island in Ontario. She has been writing and illustrating for 49 years.

← **Sindiso "R!OT" Nyoni** was born in Bulawayo, Zimbabwe, and now makes his home in Johannesburg, South Africa. He's been drawing since he was four years old, and he works in pen, ink and digital.

← **Jeannie Phan** was born in Winnipeg, Manitoba, and now lives in Toronto. She's been freelancing professionally for over four years; she's been an artist for a lifetime. She's also a horticulturalist and winner of a National Magazine Award.

↑ Artist, art teacher and illustrator **Eva Campbell** was born in Ghana. Her oil on canvas illustrations have won and been nominated for many awards. She lives in Victoria, British Columbia.

← Illustrator and designer **Loveis Wise** was born in Washington, DC, and lives in Philadelphia. She mostly creates using digital methods, graphite and gouache, and she's been an artist for as long as she can remember.

Tundra Books, an imprint of Penguin Random House Canada Young Readers,
a Penguin Random House Company

Library and Archives Canada Cataloguing in Publication

Walters, Eric, 1957-, author
     From the heart of Africa : a book of wisdom / Eric Walters.

Issued in print and electronic formats.
ISBN 978-1-77049-719-1 (hardcover).—ISBN 978-1-77049-720-7 (EPUB)

     1. Aphorisms and apothegms—Juvenile literature. 2. Proverbs,
African—Juvenile literature. 3. Conduct of life—Quotations, maxims,
etc.—Juvenile literature. 4. Sayings. I. Title.

PN6278.C57W35 2018   j398.9'96   C2017-902585-6
                                             C2017-902586-4

Published simultaneously in the United States of America by Tundra Books of
Northern New York, an imprint of Penguin Random House Canada Young Readers,
a Penguin Random House Company

Library of Congress Control Number: 2017939147

Edited by Samantha Swenson
Designed by CS Richardson with Terri Nimmo
The text was set in Harriet.

Printed and bound in China

www.penguinrandomhouse.ca

1   2   3   4   5   22   21   20   19   18

tundra | Penguin
             Random House
             TUNDRA BOOKS